W9-CFZ-009

Behind the Volcanoes

Behind the Volcanoes

POEMS

Jules Nyquist

First U.S. Edition 2014
Printed in the United States of America

Design by Jules Nyquist, Pamela Adams Hirst & Deb Coy
Text typeset in Calibri & Bodoni

ISBN-13: 978-1493685806
ISBN-10: 1493685805

Notes:
These poems previously appeared in the following publications:

Monarchs for Laura, Magnolia and Perfidy in *House Organ*
Someone Stole My Obama Sign and Hyannis Port on-line in *Duke City Fix*
Across Colors and The Lost Forty in *The Rag*
Kansas, Weep with Me and Imaginary Borders in *Malpais Review*
Behind the Volcanoes in the broadside for the *The Karen Chamberlain
        Poetry Festival,* Carbondale, Colorado
The Other Girls Wear Dresses in *Grey Sparrow Journal*
Black Phone in *Gravity of Ghosts*
First Born Brother in *Salamander* and Appetites
What is Coming and Horizons in Appetites
Somewhere in *Adobe Walls #5*
Lunar Eclipse in *Le Mot Juste*
Forest Fire in *Prometheus Chair*
Track in sketchbookproject.com

For those who have crossed – you are remembered.

For John – for being here.

`Contents

Preface

I.

II.

III.

IV.

V.

Preface

The volcanoes that sit silently on the west side of Albuquerque have surprised me with their quiet wisdom. As a newcomer, they enchanted me as much as the more noticed, and much loved, Sandia Mountains. Whenever I want to escape from the city, I drive out "behind the volcanoes" to the day use area near Petroglyph National Monument off Atrisco Vista Boulevard. The "three sisters" as we call them, are cone volcanoes and officially named "Vulcan," "Black" and "JA," plus two volcanoes a bit north, named "Butte" and "Bond." Hiking the trails and experiencing these dormant volcanoes (they are not extinct, but have been classified as dormant, which means they could erupt again) I learn that Vulcan last erupted about 150,000 years ago. The five-mile-long chain of five volcanoes lies about seven miles west of Albuquerque proper. *"New Mexico has the* largest number, range of ages, diversity of types, and range of preservation, *and some of the* best type examples of volcanoes *in the North American continent."* (quoted from the New Mexico Museum of Natural History and Science website. It's also handy when I live across the park from the Museum!)

I live on the edge of volcanoes. Albuquerque is unique in that we have such young basaltic volcanoes so close to the city. Albuquerque and our volcanoes are on the Rio Grande Rift, where the earth's crust stretches and pulls. The East African Rift and the Rio Grande Rift are two of the youngest and larger continental rifts currently active on planet Earth. Hidden in the midst of our great beauty are some of the most geologically, ecologically and interesting places.

There are also encroaching edges of death and danger. Man-made areas such as Kirtland Air Force Base, Sandia Labs, the birthplace of the atomic bomb two hours north in Los Alamos, nuclear waste buried in our desert, military jet fuel leaking into our water table, untamed forest fires, all threaten the natural beauty and environmental structures for survival. Yet in the midst of my personal experiences with the loss of loved ones, wars and grief there is transformation and healing.

The open space with the wind blowing in my face cleanses me and gives me perspective. There is more to life than just me, just us, humans on the planet. The planet itself is alive and breathing. I can hear her breath here by the volcanoes. I am enchanted and grateful to be living in a city on the edge of the volcanoes where I can see them every day on the horizon from my window. There is life at the edge of the ridge, a new view behind the volcanoes.

Jules Nyquist – Albuquerque, New Mexico
Spring 2014

I

"One knows what one has lost, but not what one may find."

-- George Sand

• • •

Behind the Volcanoes

Behind the volcanoes
there are grassy knolls
and dark emeralds.

Behind the volcanoes
lie the backsides of everything.

Broken condoms, needles, trash
of adolescent escape
long dead eruptions.

Behind the volcanoes
sits a small local airport,
with cattle grazing.

East of the Mississippi
there has been no recent
volcanic activity.

A scientist hiked to the rim of one
of our Three Sisters and proclaimed
they were not extinct, just dormant.

On a spring day I drive
the road behind the volcanoes.

Magnolia

for Cindra

We drive seven hundred miles
to meet Sylvia Plath

in the card catalog,
read *Moby Dick* in Eureka Springs.

Tarot is in the bar
with the blue impossible.
Take a chance with a difficult answer.

You dream and magnolia blossoms
appear on the boulevard.

Fragrant and thick,
openings turn to white.

Kansas

At the edge of the prairie
she is intimate with overcast sky; a small ball of sun
already low on the horizon at two p.m.

It is 38 degrees two days from home.
Christmas carols play on the radio.
Her car hangs on the black of the road

on the asphalt built by oil.
She saw her first oil well a few mile markers back,
then another, and another, continually pumping.

Semi trailers come towards her in the other lane,
followed by cars waiting to pass
like flies attached to a horses' flank.

The wind here is strong enough
to tilt trees, to make her grip the steering wheel hard
when she meets a truck in the other lane.

Frosted trees
rise out of a tan horizon
she calls the Antarctica of the West.

She's been wearing a mask for years
and hundreds of miles,
finally takes it off around Greensburg.

At a rest stop, a truck driver
waves to her from his cab,
parked on the other side of the lot.

In the distance, hundreds of ravens
swarm over the trees like bees,
fluid as one organism.

Over a hundred years ago on this same road
teams of horses carried the mail
from Wichita to Kingman pulling coaches

changing teams every eight to ten miles
until they were beat by the railroad.
They might as well have been transporting

a princess in a glass cage
or a middle-aged lover in white.
Now, sixty trains a day

haul cattle through Stone County
as the woman drives highway 54,
the old Santa Fe Trail.

Owls visit her.

Ashen and tan,
one from the side of the road
grabs prey with its talons, shows its face.

A white owl flies over her, towards her car.
It happens so fast she forgets why
she had to leave her body
in the first place,

she forgets why her body
had to be pulled into a man's,
she forgets why she needed

to be out of their blind affections
out of their dreamy lies and conversations
on winter solstice, the longest night.

She needs to race the sun,
needs to reach the Oklahoma border before
she is blinded,
needs to know in what city she will spend the night.

Hotel Crystal

In the Oklahoma panhandle
the woman from the prairie
drives until dark.

A Christmas tree glitters like grandma's jeweled brooch
in the window of the brick brownstone,
and she slows down in Boise City.

"Hotel Crystal" is such an elegant name
for a hotel
in this mile-long town.

"Forty-five a night," says the gray-haired lady
 at the front desk.
She wonders if the clerk thought up the name
to entice travelers like her.

An ancient computer monitor sits in the lobby
and the TV room is stacked with VCR tapes.
The lady invites her to browse the "library"
on the way to her upstairs room.

Paperback diet books, ten year old seed catalogs
and macramé references
barely fill the small bookshelf.

The woman plops on the bed where
anything is comfortable after eight hundred miles.
She pops off the bottle cap from the last beer in her cooler
gazes at the dark paneled rooms and striped shag orange
          carpet.

The space envelopes her in memories
of her parent's rec room
where she is twelve again,
imagines what her life would be like
when she is old enough to move out of the house.

The furniture could be out of a theater set.
She is the one watching others play her life out on stage.
She smokes a joint, watches the smoke hang in the air
and realizes this is a non-smoking room.
An imaginary man enters,
there to get her another beer
in a town with no liquor store.

The cable works, the remote is lost
and she falls asleep with the window blinds open
so she can see the stars.

She dreams of finding the lost remote
under her pillow.
Venus is watching,
brighter here than she's seen her in awhile.

Perfidy

To perforate, pierce and
facilitate
separation
is your perfunctory duty.

It is the point (at which)
I become periodically
ruined.

The perigee (around my
          earth)
widens as you orbit my body.

My perimeter is
          exposed
          as peritoneum, that smooth
          transparent membrane
          that lines the cavity of my abdomen.
Scientific thoughts react the same as cells
create rocks
to break forth as moons.

I scatter the ashes as salt on your shoes.

You are paranoid at your own peril.

Monarchs for Laura

for L. Barnes 1962-2005

When the planet seems small and you write about a man sleeping under a bridge, you ask me: is it good? I will help you with the words under water, the ocean I sought in the bay of Santa Barbara. You ask me to bring Prince in my luggage and your students in the playground ask where Minnesota is, so you take me out dancing and the guys say "do you feel the beat?" Monarch butterfly wings land on your outstretched hands, migrate to the trees with hanging moss. Tom Petty sings "Free Falling." Your husband heads out to Ventura and you take me to your stable so I can watch you ride horses. Your tan jodhpurs rub against their flesh and the weight of the mountains and I haven't seen you in fifteen years, but the letters keep coming, piling up in my closet shoebox, unclassified. An email arrives with your name as the subject, from your husband. I knew before I opened it up that you had left me here, you woke up in the trees.

The Other Girls Wear Dresses

She has Barbie dolls too, but mostly they lay naked under the bed or drive imaginary sports cars. Sometimes she papers their shoebox wall houses with leftover wallpaper or has them sit on inflatable floral pink furniture spread out on the lawn. The other girls, Pamela and Denise, come to visit and her mother wants a photo on the blanket in the grass. Pamela wears a light blue dress, her dark hair flowing, and Denise has her blonde hair tied with a bow. They pose and smile for the camera, sitting politely. She sits with them, squinting into the sun behind her baby blue cat's eye glasses, with the striped slacks her mother made for her cuffed up around her legs, her socks and dark shoes next to the girls' elegant sandals. Little brother is here with their dalmation dog ready to be the horse. Time to go, time to play cowboys and Indians.

A Kind of Courage
(sestina)

What kind of courage is it?
The anxious, scary kind,
the pottery on her aunt's shelf in turquoise blue
chipped on the rim, well-worn and loved
 through three generations and now you are
        responsible
for keeping it safe, handling it to save your life.

What kind of fool takes their life
and leaps into their unfamiliar? It's
a congested kind of dust responsible
 for new allergies, a woman who never knew the
        kinds
of desert plants that would settle her into love
 of chamisa, blooming yucca, juniper and incredible
        blue

sky, blue hovering sadness, blue
disappearing into the Great Lakes. Her life
out of the fog of waiting. How she loved
seeing Dad at the kitchen table, six am, it
was him alone, eating breakfast cereal, kindness
in his hands as she joined him, responsible

for getting up for school, responsible
with Mom and brother still in bed, her blue
 eyes join his dream world of the working trucks, kinds
of home calling her away even then. Life
someday giving her offices, cubicles, typewriters, it
 never stopped with just carbon paper and blue
        stencils loved

by her Mom's church secretary upper office, love
of the smell of mimeographed bulletins responsible
for news and prayer chains and the next holy
          season, it
churns them out around the wheel of yellow, blue,
purple, pink and red. She waits for her life
to arrive at the front steps, waits for the boy on the
          motorcycle, kind

 of coming to pick her up, where they kind
 of talk and lay down in the green park grass where
          love
eludes her young body this time. Life
will grow on in years, waiting to be responsible
for her own wedding crystal, her own blue
sky over her grandmother's lost grave in Iowa, it

takes her prairie life and leads her. A kind
of courage, it gives her love of the wind,
her response to chipped blue pottery.

II

Vortex - an indestructible node or cluster.

-- Liam Rector

The Ladies' Room

Joan enters the funeral parlor and senses Caroline's casket across the room. When her eyes finally I make contact with her friend's bloated, makeup-heavy face, abandoned men grip into her belly and the walls start to move in with the force of breaking bones on once strong joints, never fully healed, never the same again. The only thing on Joan's mind right now is to escape to the Ladies' Room. Instead, a trail of ex-husbands follow on her heels like stray puppies. One attaches himself to her like the cancer that killed Caroline, that took both her breasts, went into remission like an old lover, then came back to eat away at her brain. Joan's ex assumes a state of familiarity in his conversation that annoys her, pursues her with sly remarks like needles drawing into her skin, but her bones are stronger now, and he is a courting boy that has no chance. The other ex slides up beside her. They both know Caroline's widow, standing there in his suit, playing host. Just last week Joan saw Caroline and her husband in the hospital. She knew then, when her husband was calling Caroline "my little girl," spoon-feeding her meal, and stroking her hair that Caroline was truly domesticated. Joan tried to make her laugh, but she knew Caroline's husband would marry again before her sheets even left the house. Standing by the casket, Joan again longed for the Ladies' Room. The priest blocked the way, insisted on sharing presentable memories, proclaimed the wake a full-fledged mass, condemned the non-believers, but the miracle failed. Just then, Joan thought she heard Caroline, laughing through the bathroom door.

What is Coming

It is coming with a phone call.
You can't come to dinner, it's cancer.
Lung.
Brain.

I visit you in your bedroom in the June afternoon.
Your dad answers the door, serves us fresh squeezed
lemonade.
We have both been divorced the same number of years
and are still like sisters.

Cancer. Back from Hodgkin's decades ago.
When you started dating my brother
your hair was short and dark
from the recovery. You, sitting in the kitchen of the house
with partying bachelor boys.
A year later, married, with your long blonde hair,
the scar on your chest from the surgery.

Your boyfriend jogs down the street in the heat.
He told you the truth that he was not married,
he was the only man
you could trust.

I come back with magazines and movies.
It is something for me to do.
You have lost weight, cheeks puffy from the chemo.
When the radiation starts you will have to wear a mask and
worry about sunburn,
about seizures.
That is what scares you,
along with the bills piling up on your dresser.

Your sleek Audi is in the garage,
the silver two-seater with the stick shift
your boyfriend taught you to drive.
You walk down with me to the front door,
to see how hot it is outside.
You water the flowers, bright yellow-somethings in a pot.
It is time for me to go, for you to take a bath
while you can still walk.

It is there, waiting for us. What is coming.

I lose my body in my bathtub
weightless
I can't feel it anymore, the water is the same temperature.

I am free
from its desires
its longings.
This is what it must feel like to die, to separate,
to have no touch.
I still have feeling.
I still have love.
Still water is glass over my torso.
If I stay here, without moving, I will not break.

You enter your banquet fundraiser at the VFW
looking great in your new black outfit your daughter bought
for you: the wig, the hat, the boots.
Your son holds your hand, he is so like you.
Now 13, my nephew is silent and waiting,
for what is coming.

We sit with you at the table listening to karaoke
sipping our wine and whiskey.
You take a swig of medicine straight from the bottle.
It helps you swallow.

Lisa's Ice Cream
Ode in Six Parts

I.

I am helping you eat ice cream and your favorite is chocolate. At home you are propped up in the hospital-issued bed, and your dying body brings you back so that we treat you almost like a baby. You insist on feeding yourself. You have the bowl up to your chin, holding it with one hand, the other hand grasping the spoon as you move it slowly to your mouth. Now you can eat whatever the hell you want, the chemo and radiation have stopped and you have your appetite back. You are losing strength, but the ice cream feels good on your throat, you can still swallow. I watch you eat, bite by bite, and slowly relax out of my rushed state to cherish every remaining moment with you. With death it's okay to be here, right now, not thinking about when I have to leave or what time it is, or what I have to do. You are eating faster. Do you want another bowl? Yes. Your twenty-something daughter, my niece, brings you another one. Chocolate. I stroke your arms, your skin is so soft, your knit cap keeps your head warm. It is January and you wear a tank top and shorts and are covered with a fleece afghan. You are still beautiful at 44. Your dad is here too, sometimes he comes in to rub your feet. Your daughter has given you a pedicure and painted your toenails. I rub my own arms with the body oil spray that the hospice nurse has brought. Morphine and your daily dose of medications are delivered personally to your door, sorted by your daughter in labeled Ziploc bags.

II.

When the hospital bed replaced your bed, that's when everything changed.   No more piling on your bed, sometimes with your son or your brother, or the cat or dog, where we watched movies. I would rub your back and hug you close. I expected that you might lose the cancer battle, but it was somewhere out there in the distance. Now it is here, in the room with us. I bring my friend Karen along, we were in high school together, and you are glad to see both of us. You talk to Karen about the limo we had for the bachelorette party over fifteen years ago we are surprised at what you want to talk about. We are focused on saying our goodbyes, and you struggle to remember things.   We laugh and reminisce, and then remember we can't go out anymore like we used to. Sometimes you are afraid, and your daughter comes to your side to remind you to breathe, and listen to your body. Your body is on schedule, it is doing all the right things. "Is this Shirley's ice cream?" you ask. "No," I say, "this is your ice cream. You are home now." Shirley is my mom, and you are remembering your visits to my parents home.   When you divorced my brother we still stayed close, like sisters.

III.

I tell you how much I love you, that you are a bright shining star and that you will always be with me, you are always my friend, I will always remember you. It is my way of saying goodbye. Each time I visit it gets harder. I always think this will be the last time. Each time I hug you more, hold your hand, rub your feet, kiss your cheek. Sometimes I want to wake up and hope that it is all a bad dream. Your daughter now has your cell phone. Another piece of reality sinking in, I can no longer call you. You can barely speak. I leave that night feeling love. I always feel better after I see you. When life was getting me down, when boyfriends cancelled plans, when I wanted someone to talk to, you were there. I always knew what was going on with my niece and nephew from your updates and we were there for each other.

IV.

Four days later your daughter calls me. It is Monday, Martin Luther King Day and I have the day off work. Can I come over to see how she has fixed up your room? Absolutely. She has draped the furniture in soft colored sheets, soothing peach, tan, beige. She has lit a candle and set up a few photos. There is no clutter. I help her put a chair from the other room in the corner and cover it with a bedspread. Now we can all sit here and be with you. You are sleeping now, rarely move, your body is shutting down. I know you hear us. My nephew is downstairs in the living room, listening to his new ipod. He's 14. Your daughter is like a second mom to him, his older half-sister. She is there with her partner and we go downstairs to talk, leaving the door open a crack. We have to eat, so we order pizza. I notice how much we are in our bodies, in the world.

V.

On Wednesday morning, I wake up to a text message from your daughter. "She just passed away in her sleep...." It was dated 12:20 a.m. She tells me later that she had her alarm set for midnight to give you your medication, and she noticed you had stopped breathing. She held you for awhile, and realized you had passed, peacefully, in the bedroom, while everyone was sleeping. I can only think that we prepared the way for you so maybe it wasn't scary. She said you woke up once mentioning your "new room" draped with soft colors and you liked it. The weekend speeds by with your memorial service on Saturday and we share our memories. There are so many people, so many lives you have touched. So many things I know but also so much I didn't know about all the lives you are part of.

● ● ●

VI.

A few months later, having breakfast with your daughter, I am using you as my motivation to live my life, to do things that need to be done. I have that same good feeling after I see you daughter that I had whenever I saw you. I still worry about my nephew, but the hunger I have for life is back. I read somewhere that when the dead depart, they take away any falsehood that they might have allowed us to believe when they were alive. We who are left behind have to embark on a different life, since the dead are no longer here to help us deceive ourselves. You are here for me, and if I forget, all I have to do is remember you eating those bowls of chocolate ice cream.

• • •

Box Fan

Where do you go when you close your eyes? Tina wonders.
She stares at the big box fan in the window of the diner, the
white blades circling so fast that they are one blade, swirling
breeze and sunlight into powder that can be swept off the
floor.   She closes her eyes, facing the fan.   The blades
penetrate the darkness, spots of white confetti emerge,
spinning in circles. She can hear the whoosh of metal blades,
the smoothness of the motor, the rattling of the frame. She
feels the breeze on her face, her eyelids, her hair is blowing
back. It's supposed to be dark, why does she see whiteness?
Her eyes are closed tight, blades turn faster, swirl into specks
of light, of paper white confetti in space, spinning in circles.
Blue comes in from the corners and swirls around, red comes
when she tilts her head and keeps it there, keeps it spinning.
Faster it goes, but she can't open her eyes, she has to hit the
whiteness. What will it sound like, to pass through the light?
The white blades know. They stay silent. *"Open your eyes!"*
they whisper, *"open your eyes!"* She doesn't want to, she
doesn't want it to stop.   She's terrified of the spinning,
terrified of the fan, terrified of the rattling frame. She has to
hang on for the rush of it, hang on to hit the whiteness. Hit it
with all the force she has hidden behind her eyes. At
nineteen, what does Tina know about the whiteness, what
does she know about making it stop?

Death in the 19th and 21st Centuries
For the Hennepin History Museum
Minneapolis, MN

Death in the late 19th Century
is a capital "D"
A year of mourning
in flat, black crepe
veiled hats, gloves
and best suits in public.
Six months later, the black furs, silks and velvets
slowly appear.

A five year old girl
rocks in front of the fireplace,
clutches her favorite toy.
She is dead,
posed
for a photograph.

In another photo
a mother stands behind her infant.
Her eyes closed,
hands clenched,
fists resting on her baby's gown.
The mother is the one deceased,
her corpse posed
next to her living child.

21st Century workplace
shows no visible change of dress
to mourn a loved one.
Hidden in a single day off work,
my professor's death
is honored with a Wikipedia entry.

A colleague's death prompts me
to write a sympathy note
on her Facebook profile.
I can't move myself to remove her friendship.

The actual presence of the dead
at their own funeral is optional,
even undesirable.
Cremation is popular and
environmentally friendly.
I drive around my local cemetery.
Where are the markers I'm looking for?

Grandma's gravesite is in another state.
She calls to me from hard dirt.
Those that are cremated float
in mid-air
like lost shoes,
scattered.

Secret River
(for the poets)

The Mississippi shows herself
by waiting under the bridge.
She saves those wanting to walk on water
drowns others.

Her veil falls over the dam,
built from the sand
she eroded first.

I am married to my work
to bear my children one spoonful at a time.

Her humming knows,
and I sleep
with the fish and the rocks
and the damned.

Indestructible Sentimentia

in memory of Liam Rector

I *– Liam's Shoes*

The first thing I noticed at your funeral were your shoes.
Eight or ten pairs, rising across the steps on the altar
of St. Mark's-in-the-Bowery.
Huge shoes, at least a size 13, each one
with a lit votive candle inside.
Did you have something to do with this?
Your fashion sense of expensive shoes
and seersucker suits.
I wait for your shoes to catch on fire
for you to appear and say
this is a cruel joke.

Appropriately, it is raining lightly
with a line-up of mourners outside the church.
You would have been proud.

You wife speaks to us:
 "It wasn't depression. It wasn't a whim."
You lived life in quality versus quantity
Poetry was "the third thing" between you,
married 16 years.
Wed in Donald Hall's backyard.
Black ties and red sneakers.
The last night of your life
you donned a tuxedo with a polo shirt
had a nice dinner, asked her to dance.
Did she know you were planning to kill yourself
later that evening in your study with a gun?
She didn't say.

• • •

Your daughter reads from a prepared script.
She never got to say goodbye.
Quoted a line that you always referenced (and that I
remember from Bennington)
"Life's not fair."

Donald Hall spoke, sitting in a chair instead of the podium. He
couldn't read anything prepared, he just talked,
he sounded upset.
 You wrote letters back and forth.
Three of them arrived in the mail after your death.
 You talked about movies, clothes, shoes.

Two hours later we view photos:
 "American Prodigal #6."
White wall of St. Mark's altar above the shoes
baby and childhood photos, wife, daughter, family.
The full frontal nudity shot thrown in for good measure.

Church lights stay dark; we gather outside on the patio
with water (no drinks, no toasting).
A Bennington reunion in a way,
this sad occasion with Liam in common.
Some head out to nearby bars.
I walk back the few blocks to my hotel , the Carlton Arms,
to pick up my bag and head to Penn Station.
It stops raining.

On my way down the stairs of the Carlton Arms
I pat the red Buddha.
For what - luck? Wishes?
I leave a penny for my thoughts.

I brought along Donna Tartt's novel, *The Secret History* to read while on planes and trains. Tartt models the fictional college of Hampden after Bennington College with references to the Commons, the dorms and other Bennington landmarks. It is a murder mystery, a close knit group of six sequestered undergraduate students studying Greek philosophy. Now was a fitting time to read the book:

"We don't like to admit it," said Julian (the Greek instructor in the novel), *"but the idea of losing control is one that fascinates controlled people such as ourselves more than almost anything. All truly civilized people - the ancients no less than us -- have civilized themselves through the willful repression of the old, animal self. Are we, in this room, really very different from the Greeks or the Romans? Obsessed with duty, piety, loyalty, sacrifice? All those things which are to modern tastes so chilling?"*

Suicide gives one control of death. So what if it's illegal.

Liam and Ed and I sat around the table at the student/faculty dinner the night before graduation. Liam said when he was 17 he thought of killing himself and then decided to live the next year with no regrets and it was the best year of his life. Then he turned 18 and decided NOT to kill himself. His theme at Bennington was *"Always be Closing."* He believed in creating your own opportunities. He played the *Glengary Glen Ross* movie clip reference with the same "Always Be Closing" scene (starring Al Pacino) for each new class as kind of an initiation. No introduction. If you didn't get it right away, you'd figure it out later.

"We are sending you off as a woman of letters," said Liam, *"as a player, as a person who does not only apply for jobs but*

creates them. *As both a poet (which means maker) and as a producer."* He introduced me to the vortex - what the hell was he talking about at orientation? I wanted practical details, he jumped into a fantasy that I didn't understand - not yet, anyway. He wrote on the chalkboard:

Vortex - an indestructible node or cluster.

Thinking about it now, that describes Liam. He sucked me in to the center of the program. All or nothing. He read my poems to me on cassette tape for each packet. Said very little. My entire manuscript in his voice, now stashed away in my bedroom closet. So what if he used his grandfather's shotgun to close the scene? What is left is indestructible.

Lunar Eclipse

The highest goal that humans can achieve is amazement.

- Goethe 1810, Theory of Colors

Tonight Minneapolis transpires into rods and cones
under my pupils.
Wearing a white halo, my city offers me steps of gold.
I bike to the middle of the Stone-Arch bridge
where I pause.
Purple thoughts tangle in my wind-blown hair and
I realize, for the first time,
that if I jump off this bridge
into the weeping wake,
floating with the river glass,
it will be okay.

Full moon lies bare in the Northeast,
her white light signals my resurrection.
She bobs from the fisherman's unseen boat
in a sea of indefinite color
that lacks a word for blue.

The divine is hidden
but on this night
everyone is coming out to watch.

Resurrection is not an Instant Thing

For Seth, pastor at Walker United Methodist
Church, Minneapolis, MN

i.

I have spent an hour in a circle on a steel folding chair
in the basement of Seth's church.
He killed himself
and Reverend Greg is leading the conversation.

We hang on to anything familiar.
We don't have answers, Seth could be anywhere.

He tested openings, moved diagonally in life
like a chess piece across a board
between white and black.
Testing openings.
We all get 16 pieces.

The last time I saw Seth alive
he stopped by my house with his wife
to purchase my bookcase.

What do the dreams mean? Asks Jung
Maybe you are curled in a ball
claw at the air
travel through the floor boards.
Maybe your father calls you Judas.

In Seth's house he is with his father
goes upstairs to the bedroom closet.
Captures the King.
Free to make his move,
he acquires rope. Or was it a belt?
196 pounds equals a drop of eight feet,
enough to break his neck.

ii.

Ashes remain on the surface.
I let myself into the sanctuary at midnight
(I have a key).

Self-destruction plays
the piano.
It is me.
I keep it dark.
Touch the piano keys.
I play again
after all those childhood lessons.

iii.

At my home, frozen hamburger buns are thrown
by my husband across our kitchen floor.
My co-worker drops her baby off
before the truck crosses the median
in the rain to kill her instantly.
A friend is too young to be so sick.

The dead sit on the wooden pews,
listening.

III

"The trouble with history is that the people who really know what happened aren't talking and the people who don't, you can't shut them up."

Tom Waits

"They paid more to tap my phone than they paid me to run the Los Alamos project."

J. Robert Oppenheimer

New Year's Eve in Minneapolis

Fireworks explode.
Sound echoes in crisp cold;
bounces like bullets off the skyscrapers.

Helicopters buzz around bare treetops,
afraid
of something.

Bridges are for Jumping Off, Not Falling

In homage to the Minneapolis I-35W Bridge collapse -
August 1, 2007

Hundreds of bridges
to cross over and under.
Thousands,
in a lifetime.

Safe at work on the 16th floor,
she waits for his call.
Another ten minutes
and he would have driven under.

He watched others launch canoes
into the Mississippi.
She asks how he feels.
He tells her the cop at the coffeehouse
had cement dust on his shoes.

The next day she will know
that a co-worker was found dead in the rubble
on his drive home.

> *I dream of floods,*
> *cars floating*
> *a girl standing on the ledge.*
>
> *Who will you call*
> *if that girl was me*
> *jumping off,*
> *falling?*

If a sestina falls
what would be those six words?
bridge
collapse
last
breath
text
phone?

Media hounds descend on our city
even the President makes a visit.
Fucking politicians, all out of town anyway
leave us alone!

Bridges are for suicides
not falling
for John Berryman on the Washington Avenue bridge
over the ice
for the girl who was released from the hospital
long enough to get her keys, water her plants
pick up a few things, lock her door
and jump.

She lives on the sixth floor with a balcony.
She leans over the rail...
who would find her
dead on the pavement
in the courtyard?

John Ashbery on the Bridge Next Door

for the pedestrian bridge at the Walker Art Center,
Minneapolis, MN

Steel blue and yellow beams tell me:
      It is fair to be crossing, to have crossed.

Reading Ashbery's poem I wonder why
the architect commissioned him to place his words
on these rafters
on this bridge in Minneapolis
when Ashbery lives in New York.
Scratched-on graffiti finds my fingers
I rub them across metal, across time.

In 1948 for Dad's senior class trip
all six of them drove up from the farm into what they called
        Minneapolis: the "big city."
They fit in one car, and a couple of hotel rooms.

In the early 1950's my father lived near Loring Park
in this same neighborhood.
A few months working road construction
before I was born.
He looked out of his boarding house window
with his co-worker
before this bridge, before the museum,
before twelve lanes of roaring freeway traffic
cut the neighborhood in half.

Steel and air have changed into this crossing,
this bridge, where bronze words enclose my thoughts,
where pink slippers are tucked in the stairwell and I know
the homeless were here.

It is fair to be crossing, to have crossed.

High Bridge

The Mississippi shows herself
and waits like a veiled bride
to catch her lover's fall.
My grandfather, the bastard, tried to jump
from the St. Paul High Bridge
before I was born.
Killed my grandmother by beating her up
the day after Christmas, still pregnant.
He wound up in the hospital after his attempt with escape.
Mom visited him, she told me.
I never heard the full story.

His ex-wives are scattered in Midwestern cemeteries.
He died in Key West
in a room with money
hidden in the walls.

Blood Money

Walt Whitman wrote poems
with titles like *Blood Money*
or *Song for a Certain Congressman*
or *Wounded in the House of Friends*
the latter referencing *Doughfaces,
Crawlers, Lice of Humanity.*

Not much has changed in one-hundred-fifty years.
One century to the next fighting for freedom
and the voices of the people.

Walt was devastated
when hero- fighter-journalist Margaret Fuller
drowned off Fire Island, New York in 1850
along with her lover and child.
She admired George Sand.

I wonder what she would have thought of Minnesota Senator
Paul Wellstone, murdered in a 2002 plane crash with his wife
by the same *Doughfaces, Crawlers, Lice of Humanity*
politicians.

Voices are remembered, or forgotten,
bodies lost at sea, or in cornfields
paying for their own tombs, names etched in stone.

Grand Master's Revenge

"It is easy to see the beginnings of things, and harder
to see the ends."

Joan Didion's opening line in
"Goodbye to All That"

At the Hennepin History Museum
an old uniform is on display:
black with a band of a collar around the neck.
Whoever wears this is almost a reverend
but much more powerful.

This is the Knights Templar
The Order of the Temple
a secret society, a Soldier of Christ.

The belt boasts a silver buckle with a prominent red cross
and the insignia *"IN HOC SILNO VINEER."* Latin, maybe?
Something about *"to overcome in this."*

For hundreds of years it has been going on.

The Knights Templar were the crusades'
most feared fighters
above the law, to protect the wealth of the church.
They paid no taxes
crossed borders with freedom
 answered only to the Pope.

In the Battle of Montgisard in 1177
five hundred Templar knights won
over Saladin's army of 26,000 soldiers.
They created the first 'cheques', or letters of credit
so as not to be robbed of carrying large sums of cash.

• • •

An individual would be sworn to poverty,
but was given control of the communal wealth.

The Templars took deposits, bought land,
built churches and castles,
had their own fleet of ships and ran so many things
they could be the first multinational corporation.

Enter King Phillipe of France.
Hungry for power and the wealth of the church
he hated the Templars so much
that he removed Popes at will
until he found one who would take his orders.
The Archbishop of Bordeaux became Pope Clement V.

King Philippe, in league with his puppet Pope
set out to destroy the Templars.
He secretly arranged for all of them in France
to be arrested at dawn.
It was Friday, October 13, 1307.
Friday the 13th has been unlucky ever since.

King Phillipe charged the Templars with idolatry,
heresy, obscene rituals, homosexuality,
financial fraud and secrecy.
He obtained their confessions under torture
and seized their assets.
Dozens of Templars were burned at the stake
in the original Paris.

The puppet Pope Clement V agreed to disband
the Order of the Templars
due to public scandal.
He seized the Grand Master Jacques de Molay,
who had confessed under torture but insisted on his
innocence.

King Phillipe burned him alive at the stake in 1314
with the support of the Roman Catholic Church.

The Grand Master asked to be tied at the stake
so he could face
the Notre Dame Cathedral
and hold his hands together in prayer.
He called out from the flames before his death
that both the king and the pope
would meet him before God.

When King Philippe opened the vaults of the Templars,
the fortune was gone.
Someone had known of his plan.
King Phillipe died in a hunting so-called 'accident'
before the end of the year.
Pope Clement V died a month later.

The Templars went unprosecuted.
Future kings ignored the papal orders
or were lenient with the Templars
so they regained their feared status.

For hundreds of years it has been going on.

The scent of it is here in front of me
with this old Knight's Templar uniform
in the Hennepin History Museum.

Hyannis Port

A seagull walks from sea to land
leaving footprints
on snow and sand in January.

The tide pushes in, breaking up the ice
and I walk on the beach
in boots and winter coat.
Buried shell in the sand
has no ringing, only silence.

Behind me is the JFK Memorial.
I am walking these same beaches of Nantucket Sound
as our 35th President who said:
*"The new frontier of which I see is summed up not by what
I intend to offer the American people, but what I intend to ask
of them."*

I was a baby when he was assassinated.
Some Americans remember that day with such clarity
it shortens their breath.
A lone gunman blamed,
scapegoat
someone to quickly arrest and prosecute.
It must go deeper.

Kennedy pledged to withdraw us from the Vietnam war,
pledged to break the CIA "into a thousand pieces,"
pledged to keep America a democracy.

The concrete benches are silent, praying in a circle.
I walk around them, listening, leave my footprints.
The snowy-sandy shore is waiting.

The seagull is puffing up his feathers to insulate himself
from the cold.
I retreat to my traded house on the Cape.

At night I use the outdoor hot tub
and watch the steam rise.
Half-full moon, I see my breath.

I am nestled in the thick forest of bare trees
I wonder what it was like
to walk that beach as President in summer
to wonder if he knew he was being followed

to wonder how it was
for hundreds of years
before the white man came
before we landed a man on the moon.

*The JFK Memorial was dedicated July 8, 1966 and is
located adjacent to Veteran's Memorial Park on Lewis
Bay in Hyannis, Massachusetts.*

Dallas

"What are ya, some kinda nut?!"
Carol Burnett pulls a gun on Julie Andrews
dancing around in their fringey chaps
in the musical "Big D"

A city with no river, no port
no natural resources of its own
no reason for being
except for big oil
self-made and self-segregated men.

Affluent housewives
with time and money on their hands
use politics
as an outlet for attention.

Howdy, Howdy
"Welcome Mr. Kennedy!"
proclaims the Dallas Morning News.
"Wanted for Treason" pamphlets circulate
before his arrival so is it no surprise
when the President arrives he remarks to Jackie
we're in "nut country"
moments before his death.

Fifty years later, Dallas,
your burning sun glints
off Texas hats, shady eyes
remnants of who shot J.R.
the Cowboys franchise and those glittery cheerleaders
a freshly painted Dealey Plaza.

Your commemoration ceremony
is a big jet-show flyover
the Naval Academy Men's Glee Club
and a speech by a historian.
Kennedy's legacy with spectacle
over substance.

Is there sorrow in your lies
or will we still call you "Nut Country"?

from the New York Times article
"The City With a Death Wish in Its Eye -
Dallas' role in Kennedy's Murder"
James McAuley, November 16, 2013

Before

I.

His voice
holds me
on the phone
stops me heavy between my sheets.

My legs part
to hear him.
I oversleep.
He wakes me up,
we were going to meet
for our affair, my lover
says

someone
flew a plane
into a building. Any
other Tuesday I would wonder

why would that matter? I open
my mouth but nothing
comes out. Turn
on the TV he says.
He is okay
that I am tired;
he walks away.

II.

Boxes
scatter across
the lawn I came back to.
My separated husband was just another house.

I hesitate
to move back in with the man
I married. I suspend my desires.
The voice on the phone flows back
between my black space

before
my broken lease.
He holds me down
to my guilt.

A horrible
weekend to move.
I know
it's only temporary,
I know
I will walk
away.

Eulogy: the Day After

She jumped from the 81st floor
to escape flames and smoke
of certain death
to land in comforting arms of sky and air
to live one last breath of blue
to meet her Maker face-on.

The cell phones ring one last time
on this side of the world, saying:
"I'm here, I'm hostage, I love you."

Split in two; will souls walk away
from the devastation and rubble, hang in mid-air
call those who can't hear:
"we are gone, but we still hear your hearts beating."
The dead have no boundaries now,
they can go anywhere.

You will try and find us;
pebbles and sand in an archaeologist's sieve
looking for granules of hope.
We, left behind have to remember.
We, left behind have to spread
more words around the ashes

White papers flutter around in the air like feathers;
charred edges.
The gaping hole in hearts.
The empty cavity of space in the city that calls us home
 leaves us in a vacuum.

The dead will confront us, for they have cleared the path.
They have risen out over the moon,
here over the parking lot,
over the horizon, from slivers, to halves,
to full, to new.
We all share the same moon rising.

Memory in Two Places

Memory sticks in two places: his and hers.
They sit at the kitchen table
        darkness outside an empty glass window
Individually, they are close.
Each carries expectations, separate
        living in memory
in love with painted images.

Blurry
        she removes her glasses
rests in softness
        watercolors and pale shades
until she is draped in darkness, in her own secrets.
She dreams in the middle of the day.
She touches
uses skin to see.

Static creeps, smothers his ears
he removes his hearing aid, listens to his heartbeat.
Softness rests.

Ringing grows louder, tinnitus
it never goes away. Well, maybe running water like the
        shower
or an explosive orgasm
calm spaces open to vistas, endless
        blue in a field of hills.
He hears the voices
of land
        of   skin
            of her.

Touching, they grow together
in paint.   Their only memories

• • •

inside their heads
Instead of sharing, they imagine other faces
beyond them, during sex
she makes love without him
on top of her
he goes beyond his eyes
to feel only death
he cannot get past her ghost
he fucks his pain away until he gets high
         off his coming
                  his coming inside her.

Arachnophobia

At the Trinity site the morning of the blast
scientists observed tarantulas the size of tennis balls
crossing the road.

Is my fear of spiders any excuse
to wish for the death of innocent creatures?
How can I be selective for wanting to save the lives of
        snakes
and all furry things but be depressed
because cockroaches will outlive us all?
If we had to bomb the Germans or parts of Europe
would we have done it instead of bombing Japan?

Japanese were hinting at surrender
too risky to invite them to the test.
What if it didn't work? How would we save face?

Los Alamos physicists jumped for joy
when the Fat Man test was successful.
Years of work to discover that they really could claim
the law of physics.
Uranium and later manufactured plutonium exceeded all bets
that were placed on how many tons of TNT would explode.
Lucky guy who got the highest bid: 18,000 tons.
The baby, sold to our military, grown-up gadget
 thrown into the world.

Then we dropped it.
Twice.
We didn't have to, American ego
had to beat the Russians to claim sole victory over Japan
in winning the war.
The Air Force projected vague numbers of how many distant
        insects may be destroyed (the Reds, the Yellow Peril,
        the cockroaches of civilization)

. . .

on the other side of the world.

Watching the film later of the destruction
caused by the gadget
leveling whole cities and innocent children,
tears come to the eyes of scientists.
We actually used it.
Six-tenths of a gram of pure energy with 80,000 deaths
and eighty percent of buildings destroyed from Little Boy's
       blast.

Oppenheimer was accused of being a Soviet Agent
by his own hysterical country he worked to defend.
Didn't want us to build the H-Bomb, the Super,
more and more powerful ones inconceivable at the time
we just wanted the device to end all wars.

At the Trinity site, the ants go on burrowing
and bring up tiny grains of Trinitite
that blue-green glass that is now illegal to pick up.
Visitors allowed twice a year so our biggest enemy,
amnesia, won't forget.

Why not?

for the two Afghanistan teenagers in love - NYTimes,
July 30, 2011.

Two lovers.
What right do they have
to marry someone they love?
An angry mob of 300 people surges around them,
calls them adulterers, wants them stoned to death, or
        hanged.

These two unmarried seventeen-year olds
are in love.
Embarrassed to talk about it,
they can speak plainly of one thing:
they are ready for death.

Her father wants to kill them both
when they are out of prison.
They have shamed their families
 by having sex outside of marriage,
falling in love without family approval is a crime.

Young hearts do not know boundaries
of neighborhoods or religion.
She wanted to continue her six years of schooling
but was put to work
by her family at an ice cream factory.
That's where they met.

Now, both in juvenile prison, he is beat up
with blood-laced eyes.
She is going to classes to learn how to tailor clothes.
Her cousin was killed in the riot.

Her angry family blames her, and offers her marriage
to another son to clear her debt.
As if she can love another son.

Her illiterate father visits her in jail but says nothing.
Blood, he says, is the only answer, and not with his hands,
the government's.

The boyfriend says he feels bad and prays to God to give her
back to him.
"I'm ready to lose my life."
The girlfriend says, "We are all human, God created us from
one dirt.
Why can't we marry each other, or love each other?"
Why not?

Imaginary Borders

We are tourists and U.S. Citizens driving on New Mexico
Highway 22 towards the Tent Rocks
when a ROAD CLOSED sign surprises us.
A U.S. Immigration Border Patrol station spans the road
behind a detour sign.
We drive around and notice "Mexico" on the other side in
red, green and black.

How is this possible?
It must be a movie set, the only explanation
 we can think of.
We are near Pueblo de Cochiti
Crossing pueblo land, government land,
private land, sacred land

We drive the gravel road
climbing precarious curves to the top of the mesa
I wonder if the gray clouds in the distance
 will bring rain and flash floods
leaving us stranded.
The overlook is named for American Veterans
and we walk the loop trail
as lightning flashes make me uneasy.

Am I trespassing in this place of indescribable beauty?
Volcanic ash piles from eons ago hold songs
from the women of Cochiti, the storytellers.
They echo through the spirals
preserve heritage I have lost.

On our drive back we approach a red pickup truck
stopped in the middle of the gravel road.
We wait awhile, then move to pass.

* * *

The woman is praying, she tells us through her open window.
We know now we can stop being tourists.

On our pretend entry out of Mexico,
we are free to return to Albuquerque
unlike the thousands who try to cross that border daily
unlike the real wall building into something unimaginable.

Cipriana Jurado I Hear You

Cipriana Juarado spoke at the Albuquerque Center for Peace and Justice on August 31, 2011

Seven thousand murdered women
in Cindad Juarez this summer
killed for their features, or their face, their sex,
or burned alive in their own homes
by their own people
or drug runners
or organized crime.
Mexican police protection doesn't matter
when killers cut off right hands
of the living or nipples of corpses.

Cipriana Jurado tells her story,
it is necessary for us to hear her words,
be in her presence, feel what it is like
to be in the U.S. on political asylum
with her family left behind, torn by guilt,
she feels like a traitor.

A phone call to relatives
reveals they got another loved one this week.
The perpetrators know from experience
they will not be prosecuted
for execution style killings.
Human rights activists protest publicly
and are kidnapped by the military or murdered.
Whole families gone.

The Human Rights Center was raided without a search
            warrant
by Mexican Federal Police. Files ransacked.
 Death threats.
Nineteen activists murdered in the state of Chihuahua.
Cipriana has asylum but the U.S. is not blameless,

we are the ones that have encouraged this madness.
She has to wait 150 days to get a work permit,
relies on the kindness of strangers
and human rights workers.
It is good she is here, she is telling,
Her words reach me in Spanish, translated into English
through a portable headset
so our comrades can all listen at once.

Fifty thousand murders in Mexico over the last five years.
Neither the Mexican nor US government
will recognize Cipriana or the others
because then they would have to admit
that these horrors are happening,
that they exist, that she exists.
Cipriana Jurado, I hear you.

Someone Stole My Obama Sign

Who did this? A tourist?
Left the metal frame, took the plastic sign
from my front yard
Was it an upset Catholic? Days before there were groups
of tramping, flag-carrying anti-abortion demonstrators
in Tiguex Park.   Hispanics? Blacks? Whites?
Agree to disagree but don't take my sign.
Put up your own damn sign.
You take, take, take but don't know how to give.
Cuts and cuts
and seize with greed and leave an empty frame.
Vacant, the space is still there.
Another sign will go up.
This time on my balcony, out of reach.
I already voted. No matter what candidate wins,
my sign will be here.
The moon still shines full and low
over the mountains. No one can take that away.

Weep with Me

No children in the park today.
Twenty kindergartners killed in Connecticut
The young gunman rages in a shooting spree
Kills himself and leaves us helpless
My anger drifts into the wind
As I walk in my neighborhood park

Weep with me, soil
Weep with me, sky

No more waiting for the right time to talk about this
Our tragedies multiply, it's time to acknowledge
How we treat our children
Remember our genocide on U.S. soil
That seeps up deep from the ground

Please, Mr. President, I'm waiting for you
To help pass laws to protect us from guns
To protect our children, to heal our revenge.

Even the sky is in mourning with clouds hanging low.
Vigil in the park with candles and luminarias
Helps us stand in silence
The drum beat softly comforts me and grows to
Call up my anger, call up our collective outrage.

Christmas lights still proclaim joy for an infant
To save us.
We can only save ourselves.

Money

Reverse Sestina

Money built
I tower
of a built
tower money of
and I tower
of I
a money built
of a built
money I tower
a money tower
I built of
money, I
of built tower
and I built
a tower of money.

Moon

It's three a.m.
The moon knows
the truth.

Lines for Chekhov's *Uncle Vanya's* Fortune Cookies

You ought to have done something that mattered.

The land is getting poor and more hideous every day.

Let yourself go for once in your life.

You're not mad, you're simply a crank.

I believe it's normal for a man to be a crank. You are perfectly normal.

You shall live through a long, long succession of days and tedious evenings.

You've ruined my life. I have not lived! I have not lived!

In the whole of this province there have been only two decent, cultured people -- you and I.

Wherever you go, you bring along destruction with you.

The life itself is tedious, stupid, squalid.

You used to be an inspiring personality who never inspired anybody.

Man is endowed with reason and creative power so that he can increase what has been given him, but up to the present he's been destroying and not creating.

When I'm in this state I get extremely provocative and audacious.

You will draw up the most far-reaching plans for the future!

You will marry for love, or for what at the time seemed real love.

A talented man can't stay free from blemishes in Russia.

You will fall head over heels in love with some water-sprite.

Life has swallowed you up, poisoned your blood with its putrid vapors until now you will become just as petty as all the rest.

You shall know a life that is bright and beautiful. You shall rest!

IV

*"If I go to sleep and don't wake up, other people will know I'm
dead. But I won't know it."*

Margaret Randall
(from "Albuquerque")

across colors

between pixeled squares
besides shades of orange and brown
beyond green, white, blue
during printing, blurred, smudged
in front of framed art
instead of photos
off – on – reboot
over checkerboard squares
through insect eyes
toward primal universe
underneath sand
up
to a new horizon, crawl on your knees
          scrape, bruise
within
without your eyes to tell
          you your truth
on paper
on chips
nearly reality
about nothing tangible
across colors, harmony blends

Black Phone
For my grandmother

The old black phone rings
with a long, hollow bell sound – bbbrrrringggggg
The phone company came to replace it with the up-to-date
       model.
The woman lifts up the receiver from its base,
substantial in her hand
holds it to her ear and answers
"Hello?"

On my end she's been dead 70 years
In her time, she hears my faint voice of the future.
Her husband hollers, "Who is it?"
"No one, static," she says.
 He doesn't believe her
gets up and grabs the receiver from her
"Hello?" He asks, "Who is this?"
I listen, as he hears only the blackness between us
and hangs up.

Horizons

I dreamed you cut your hair. Your neck, white and smooth, says the new life will be easier. The necklace would have been best kept under glass. Turquoise stones circle your neck. The travel brochure mentions silence three times. You ask the devil for a new type of bondage.

The turquoise encounters your hidden grave. Why does she see it now, hidden from view for over sixty years? They pray for you. Carpenters keep hammering. You close your eyes. A man climbs up on the roof. A woman disappears into thin air. You say a spell upon waking. Horizons keep rising every twenty-four hours.

Your exposed skin can be touched only in circles. The tortoise buries herself in the sand. Don't feel pity, name the stones on your neck instead, touch them in the dark. What do I say when I see your empty shell on the beach? I squeeze your hand. They've made you into a bowl, turned you upside down, hung you on the wall.

For my grandmother, Margaret Adelaide Keppler Lindberg
who was murdered by my grandfather due to domestic
violence and died December 26, 1939 at the age of 26. She is
buried in Fort Madison, Iowa.

I Called You Grandma

At ten I sewed my clothes
in the basement.
Pulled threads through the eye of the needle
on my mother's machine.

You were the lady across the street
with the large doll on display
in the corner of your living room.
Gathering fabric
for the daughters you never had.
You dressed my mom, the blonde, in blue
and her sister, the brunette, dead at 33, in pink.

At the department store when I was twenty,
you asked me what I liked in a new machine.
Said it was for you,
and after you paid for it, said it was for me.
I made my wedding dress four years later.

You saw photos of the dress with the blue ribbons in the hospital
before you died.
You were too sick to come to the ceremony.
When the doll fell over,
divorce ripped my seams,
the thin threads broken.

First-Born Brother

Dad scrapes out the overgrown grass around your grave
with a butter knife
plants marigolds around our last name.

Mom quit her job for your arrival,
delivered you into the ground.
I was not the eldest, after all.

We sit on the couch,
your baby ink footprints in my lap,
our feet unable to touch the floor.

Dad's Hunting Rifle at Christmas

At my parents house, gifts are opened
except for the hidden one behind the tree.
Dad reaches for it, says to my husband:
"you might appreciate this."

He unzips the well-worn cloth case
to reveal the old hunting rifle, one of many Dad had
from the late 1950's or early '60's.
It was used up north where Dad and Frank
brought back a deer and a Christmas tree
 tied on top of the car.
Blondie, our golden lab trained for birds,
brought in duck, pheasant and grouse.

My husband will take the old rifle home with us
to accumulate in his basement gun safe.
He will leave with the boys in his truck for a week
of hunting deer and drinking,
leaving me with the dog that doesn't hunt
and a garbage bag of empty beer cans.

His handgun is hidden on the upper shelf of the bedroom
            closet.
Loose bullets in the nightstand drawer
float around with keys and spare change.

I fear he will kill himself with one of the guns
which wouldn't be all that bad
but I don't want to be around if he does it.

Watching the Sunset with Dad on the Deck in the Ozarks Overlooking Table Rock Lake

We talk of crows.
Their cackling gossip
scatters across the oak trees.

Tiny lizards crawl out of cracks
between the boards to warm themselves
in the sun. I try to catch one

and you say, "throw a towel over him."
Blue hills up and down the hollow,
wear mown strips of cut trees. Power lines

tattoo the hilltops. The locals call the
scalped hills *baldknobbers*
and turkey vultures glide low on the rising air.

I count five, six, then seven of them.
They swoop in, and I squirm in my chair.
You say they smell natural gas line leaks.

They float in spirals, signals
for the energy company.
The stealth bomber base is just miles away
and the 5 & 10 sells Confederate flags.

Tar paper shacks dot the backroads
and Jesus runs for office. His name is on
lawn signs all over the place.

We sit side by side, father and daughter.
Here is where you retire,
far enough away to have out of state plates.

V

"There is an exuberance and lavishness about the foliage that is intoxicating and the lascivious plentitude of their form fills me with primitivism..."

--Wanda Gag

"I wish people were all trees and I think I could enjoy them then."

--Georgia O'Keeffe

● ● ●

Forest Fire

From the headline: "Hint of Normalcy in Colorado Springs" – Albuquerque Journal, July 1, 2012. Names have not been changed.

In the heat of summer, retiree Nina Apsay loads the mounted deer heads into her Hyundai SUV. She evacuates with caribou antlers piled on top of a few suitcases. The antelope head is her prized possession. It stares at her with its glass eyes in the suburban neighborhood with winding streets and split-level homes as she pulls out onto the interstate. This time the fire wins, the winds blow close enough to drench her home in smoke, and this time she knows the fear of pending death. She feels the weight of the loaded rifle in her hands. Her trophy mounts bring her closer to nature, closer to control. When her husband died, this was all she had left of their times on the range together. National Guard soldiers help police the roadblocks to lead her, along with the 30,000 other residents, out of the city. She flocks to safety, doing what she is told. Suddenly, the antelope head leaps through the window of Nina's SUV. It races up the mountainside and is consumed by flames. It will not be trapped or mounted any longer. The stuffed deer heads follow, slide right through the SUV glass! Live deer watch them from the meadow that is still safe, watch the antelope head and deer heads, followed by the caribou antlers, as they all leap and roll themselves into the forest fire. Nina doesn't notice that her stuffed animal heads are missing. She won't notice anything until she stops for the night and realizes they are gone, leaving her with the empty wooden mounts piled on top of her suitcases. She will blame it on vandalism. She knows that's impossible since she never left her vehicle. She chooses the easy answer, the one she wants to believe, that the deer in the meadow watching from across the freeway are there for her viewing pleasure. They stare at her in the smoky night.

* * *

Somewhere
(sestina)

This is the somewhere
We were always trying to get:
Landscape
Reduced to the basics:
Rolling mills, rocks, running
Water, burdocks, trees living and dead. (1)

Somewhere the dead
are buried under humps of dirt, somewhere
a white cross perches with faded plastic flowers run
over on the highway by drivers who will rush to get
somewhere unimportant. A basic
necessity of burial: warm landscape

soft enough to dig. We walk the land, scope
out our future with planted trees, no dead
ancestors among us. Basic
survival skills are burdock roots, some
flower stalks harvested before they get
to bloom. Tree bark stripped off as runners

to make canoes, stone faces stare at us from the bank. We
       run
into landscape.
Some day we will elope to a new place, get
dressed in red and tie ourselves to trees. The dead
and living surround us. Somewhere
in our pockets lie changes. BASIC

programs run on a green screen. Basic
codes run all life forms. Somewhere someone runs
deep into the forest. Ferns unfold.   Some ask where
they are but we see another landscape
appear on the screen. Death
sleeps under down covers. No graveyards to get

creepy with. Graves are fine and private, we get
consolation in the land of Elysian, a basic
right of passage with manicured lawns, the dead
no longer gone but sweetly singing under running
water, weeping willows, the statuary landscape
attracting tourists with guidebooks, draped urns, winged
          cherubs, somewhere

over the rainbow death got lost.
This is the somewhere we exit, back to basics.
Run to the stonecutter, chisel our own mortality.

1 – opening stanza quote is verbatim from "Daybooks 1," Two
Headed Poems, Margaret Atwood 1978.

Girl as Tree

Her delight is in the woodlands
she paints the world
unfurling green strokes

turns humans into ferns,
gathers them in groups under shade
so they are incapable of killing.

Her name is Daphne,
the naked one.
Her arms are brilliant green branches,
her hair, tendrils of red bark.
She was born underground
in a hive of dirt.

A woman from her neck down,
her face becomes a tree-top,
retains leaves of orange and red.
In winter she sheds her leaves to reveal
the veins of her heart,
unable to face the demands of love.

She runs within the forest,
her feet black and worn
just out of reach of the man that pursues her.
She asks the earth to enclose her
and her limbs become stiff,
her feet stick to the ground like roots.

She is transforms her body into a tree
sits in the forest,
always out of reach.

The man kisses the wood of her,
asks her to be his tree,
but she is one with the roots now,
in the safety of dirt.

Sometimes the storms pass through the forest,
thunderous and heaving.
How many names will they take?

She is afraid of love, that only truth.
She is afraid of humans, with their flames of fire.
Some men forget they were ferns,
they have forgotten where they came from
and prophesize of days when they will rule the world.

The man returns to the forest,
He can only think of Daphne,
the girl as tree.
Her ears are knots in the wood,
He strokes her branches
brings offerings of pure water.

Blue and green leave the sky
so it is once again black as dirt.
Daphne rises up on her trunk to embrace
the night, reaching her roots
as deep below as she does above.

Daphne starts wondering when she can start
being a woman again and rest against a tree.
The man kneels at her feet
to massage the stiffness out of her.
He asks the earth to release her,
so he can take care of her.

The man who loves her calls her name
and Daphne rises up out of her trunk
to embrace him.

This time she will stand beside the man.
Woman as tree.

The Lost Forty

For the trees at "The Lost Forty" in the Chippewa
National Forest near Grand Rapids, Minnesota.

Here, where the red and white pines
are four hundred years old

We smoke and sit
at the foot of the thickest trunk,

rough bark against my back.
The ferns make me feel primitive.

We talk about how they move,
send out seeds.

They invade the space slowly.

I lie down in their greenness
to watch the sky.

Spaces of blue fill emptiness.
Trees do not feel despair.

They throw out numbers of themselves,
reproduce without touch.

Male and female pinecones,
Mushrooms, moss.

I write down what they say.

Blue Trees Fly

blue trees fly
drift among clouds
cottonwoods and pines together
lacy branches weave a place of protection
they cry at night
tears with stars
float in space
invite me to sit
where they once had roots

Magdalena

Near Magdalena, the mountains are like ocean waves
sculpted in stone.
153 miles and we forget to bring beer.

Your college friend meets us at the post office,
handsome as ever in his long-sleeve shirt
and khaki pants,
an upstate New York academic
living on a make-believe ranch.

We follow him in his white pickup
paved roads turning to dirt, sailing into the high seas
where we finally reach his tidy, book-filled house with
triangular views of the mountains.

For lunch, we have a choice of several Progresso soups
and bottled beer to quench our thirst.
Out here, fresh produce is a half day's drive
unless you grow it yourself.
I admire the photos of fellow poets displayed
on the upper ledge of the kitchen cabinets,
and assume he knows most of them personally.

He has a bed with a red spread
a bachelor pad, and I wonder
if he sees a woman's face in the mountains
or maybe Mary Magdalene as his mother.

After lunch we hike the arroyo.
I'm in my street boots and stumble on rocks
 unprepared with improper footwear.
Watch out for rattlesnakes! he laughs
and we know he is not joking.

Juniper trees spread their gnarly, dry branches
in front of me.
I could be in a biblical land
with endless sand dunes
sprinkled with sage
a lost disciple.

You wait for me and lend your hand
as we work our way through the wilderness.
Mother Mary, majestic in your mountain,
deliver us.

Track

Ballooning we hover
over train tracks at sunset, out by Laguna.
BNSF half-mile long, cars hauling uranium.

Just me and the pilot landing in the casino parking lot.
Mostly old people (but some young ones)
where money is traded for dreams.

Six thousand dollars is counted out to one woman
in cash, hundreds.
Time to get out of here.

City lights a distant flicker on the horizon
we float east and the train is still there, motionless.
I think of my parents, they would like this adventure.

They sleep three states away, distant.
Dreams so deep they won't remember
the journey when they wake up in their room.

The pilot gives us a shot of propane.
We rise, reaching;
content to drift,
silent at sunrise.

ABOUT THE AUTHOR

JULES NYQUIST lives in Albuquerque, New Mexico and is the founder of the Poetry Playhouse. She leads creative writing classes and invites visiting poets to share their work. She took her MFA from Bennington College, Vermont and her previous poetry collection, *Appetites,*(Beatlick Press) was a finalist for the New Mexico/Arizona 2012 Book Awards. Her website is www.julesnyquist.com (Photo by John Roche)

ABOUT THE PRESS

 **BEATLICK PRESS** was established in 2011 to honor the memory of Beatlick Joe Speer of Albuquerque, New Mexico and continue his artistic mission to publish deserving writers:

BEATLICK PRESS

Pamela Adams Hirst, publisher
Beatlick Press
45 Garden Park Circle NW
Albuquerque, NM 87107
www.beatlick.com

Other Publications by **BEATLICK PRESS**:
"Writers with something to say"

Backpack Trekker: A 60s Flashback: Beatlick Joe Speer
  2013 NM/AZ Book Awards Finalist: Travel
Beyond the End of the Road: Deborah Woodside Coy
Straw: Carol Moscrip
Appetities: Jules Nyquist
  2012 NM/AZ Book Awards Finalist: Cookbook
The Philosophy of God's Mind: Paul A. Speer
Down Time to Tombstone: David Tammer, David Lavar Coy
La Llorona: An Anthology Deborah Woodside Coy
  2013 NM/AZ Book Awards Winner: Anthology
My Season of Grief: Pamela Adams Hirst
Events You Design: Teresa Speer
Bubblegum Box: A Children's Book: Deborah Woodside Coy

Made in the USA
San Bernardino, CA
11 May 2014